*www.magentasunhealing.com*

*Contact Chloe by email at*
*chloe@magentasunhealing.com*

*First paper edition: October 2022*
*Edited and written by: Chloe Moers*

*Copyright © 2022 by Chloe Moers*
*All rights reserved. This book or any portion thereof*
*may not be reproduced or used in any unintended*
*manner whatsoever*
*without the written permission of the author*
*except for the use of brief quotations.*

*The publisher and the author make no guarantees*
*concerning the level of success you may experience by*
*following the advice and strategies contained in this*
*book, and you accept the risk that results may differ*
*for each individual.*

Learn the Art of Channelin

# **_Table of Contents_**

| | |
|---|---:|
| Intro | 4 |
| What is Channeling? | 6 |
| Protection and Safety | 9 |
| Grounding | 15 |
| Unconditional Love Energy | 23 |
| Activating a Merkaba Field | 30 |
| Raising Your Vibration | 36 |
| Various Beings, Essences, Consciousnesses | 44 |
| Surrender and Trust | 46 |
| What Does Channeling Feel Like? | 49 |
| Different Forms of Channel Expression | 52 |
| Cleansing Your Channel | 57 |
| Entering the Heart Space Method | 60 |
| Entering the Heart Portal Method | 72 |
| Above the Crown Method | 78 |

| | |
|---|---|
| Beside You Method | 84 |
| Within Another Method | 90 |
| Channeling is Limitless | 96 |
| Conclusion | 98 |
| About the Author/Channeler | 100 |

# **Intro**

Welcome to this course on learning how to channel. In it, you will find guidance on how to connect with, communicate with, and channel positive beings, energies, higher selves, spirits, essences, spirit guides, consciousnesses, and more.

You are loved, seen, heard, and appreciated. There are limitless beings here and present to spread light and reawaken love within the hearts of each and every life and essence.

Take your time, be present, and notice how you feel in each experienced moment. There is no rush to the finish line, the moment is now so live it.

If you have any questions at any time, you can reach out to me via email at **chloe@magentasunhealing.com**.

Below you will find channeled information on grounding, protection, connecting with love force energy, activating a Merkaba field, how to let go, how to channel and communicate using many methods in various ways, and you will learn to connect with source in a deeper way.

Recognize that this course only contains guidelines and you can always change wording and exercises to however resonates with you.

Enjoy. Love and light on. You are doing beautifully on your path!

# What is Channeling?

Channeling is the art of connecting with a being, essence, consciousness, and/or spirit in order to temporarily merge with them in a safe manner to provide healing, knowledge, art, and so much more.

There are various ways to channel and many ways to express. You may channel speak, write, dance, create, heal, move, or solely experience.

In this class, know that you are always safe and protected. The most important thing to remember is to always set your intention for the greatest and highest good and to be aware that if for whatever reason you would like to abruptly stop channeling, you are easily able to disconnect from the being you were channeling.

You are safe to let go, to positively surrender, and to open your heart to new and awakening experiences and information.

Channeling can include mediumship but is different from mediumship in the way that mediumship is focused solely on communication with spirits. Channeling can include beings in physical form (in other dimensions, realms, planes, or places), consciousnesses, higher selves, spirit guides, animals, and essences. It is not limited to just connecting with those who have passed. Through channeling, not only do you have the ability to communicate with various beings, but you can also temporarily merge with them for a variety of purposeful experiences.

It is common for people to channel in their day-to-day life. This can sometimes be interpreted as being in a "flow state" or by receiving a vision or pull. Many artists have channeled to bring forth new art forms and perspectives. Many writers have channeled stories from around the universe. Many healers have channeled energy sources and consciousness to integrate interdimensional and universal forms of healing on Earth (like Reiki). Channeling is part of our nature and is natural for all life. It can be tapped into naturally during extreme moments- including life or death situations and euphoric episodes.

All you are learning in this class is how to tap into your natural ability to channel intentionally and purposefully.

Your channel is connected from source above through source within and into source below (Earth). All you are doing is embracing your natural potential for bringing new life, energy, and awareness to Earth.

Experience forward and open your heart to love and wisdom.

# Protection and Safety

You are naturally safe and protected. The more love you feel within you, the more love you naturally will attract and receive.

The stronger your energy within is- the more connected to source you are- the less likely it is for any entity to attempt to attack or attach to you in any way. Entities feed off of fear and fear-created emotions- such as hate, resentment, anxiety, and intense stress. If you are not experiencing these things, they will have no interest in you as your light is too strong for them to get close to without them being transformed into their original love-centered selves. All beings- including ones that may come off as negative are founded on a core of love. All are derived from source which is founded on love.

A being may have become corrupted by fear and lost touch with their inner love creating a disconnection from the love that surrounds. This is what could potentially create a "negative entity". When you call upon and send the purest of love back to the core love of any being, it will transform them back to their light-origin selves. Love is the greatest transformer and is stronger than fear could ever be. True love transforms all back to their core light-filled selves.

If you were to become afraid or connect to a fear-based emotion and some entity were to attach to you, just know that calling upon pure Unconditional Love Energy (that you will be downloading soon in this class) and asking for the angels and this pure love to connect to the love within the core of the entity and transform them back to their love-centered self, will automatically work to transform them.

It is very unlikely for you to experience an attack to begin with, but know that if it were to happen, it is very easy to heal, release, and transform the "attacker". Nothing is solely how it seems and healing/transformation is much easier and flows stronger than many may believe. All energy and beings feel the best when connecting to love and re-awakening their origin self. Naturally, energy (which we are all made out of) wishes to flow back to the state that resonates the greatest. It is much harder to stay in fear (for all) than to re-awaken and re-connect with love.

It is also important to recognize that you may experience fear-based emotions from time to time and even chronic low vibrational emotions at times. You can still remain protected at these times easily and effectively. To do this, you can call upon your higher self, spirit guides, the angelic beings who are here to provide assistance, Mother Earth, unconditional love consciousness, source, and anyone else that resonates with you. Calling upon them can be said with, "I call upon my higher self, spirit guides, the angelic beings who are here to provide assistance, Mother Earth, unconditional love consciousness, and source to provide protection, true love, guidance, and support for the greatest and highest good."

Another natural act of protection is your Merkaba field. When activated, you can ask your Merkaba field to filter out certain energies, protect you from energy parasites and entities, project love outwards and inwards, and help elevate you to where you need to be. Talking towards your Merkaba field as you would a trusted friend is beneficial. Your Merkaba field is conscious and follows your intentions while also always providing what is for the greatest and highest good. If you ask your Merkaba field to do something that does not resonate, it will not. Soon, I will show you how to activate and maintain your Merkaba field.

Grounding to the heart of Mother Earth and connecting to your higher self and to source are also natural ways that you can protect yourself. When you are centered in love, light, and life, you are naturally protected. I will show you tips and ways to ground very soon.

In addition, if you feel called to do so, you can call upon a bubble of energy to surround your being with the intention of this energy to protect you and your energy fields and be a filter for non-beneficial energy. Your intention is your manifestation. If you choose to do this, you can either visualize this bubble (I like to visualize a purple amethyst color and golden light surrounding me) or you can call upon this bubble to form. Purple is typically a strong energy color associated with elevation, spiritual awakening, connection, and protection. Gold elevates beneficial frequencies, protects, and strengthens one's natural abilities and inner love-centered strengths.

I hope this information was helpful for you. Know that trust and intention are the most important. Sometimes things that may seem negative are not actually negative so asking yourself, "how does this feel and how does this resonate internally?" is very important. Try not to include personal bias based on looks as much as you can. Sometimes those that look scary are actually quite kind and sometimes those who may appear angelic are actually quite vampiric. Follow and open your heart, increase your intuition, trust and surrender to love and you shall always find your way.

Also, it is okay to have challenging experiences sometimes as they can create personal learning and growth and are not always as negative as we may interpret them to be. Always ask yourself, "what is the purpose of this experience and feeling?" Asking yourself questions is just as important as asking others questions. Continuous learning is continuous growth. Remain open and love on.

# **Grounding**

Grounding centers the body and mind. It allows for increased mental and energetic clarity. It allows for the past to be let go of and for the ocean of emotions to settle into gentle waves.

It allows you to tap into how your body, mind, soul, and spirit are feeling at this moment and it brings you back to the ever-evolving present.

It is highly recommended to ground daily, whenever you feel unbalanced, and before every connection, communication, and channeling session. The length of time for grounding varies on how you are feeling at that moment and that day. Some days you are already grounded and other days you may need an hour. Always follow your intuition with this and know that it is important to center and there is always time to do so.

There are many different ways to ground yourself. You can walk, lay, run, intuitively dance, or stand outside barefoot. You can also eat grounding foods, such as nuts and seeds, and bring your full focus and attention to these foods as you're consuming them.

Cold water is also very grounding. Taking a short cold shower or having a quick dunk in cold water in nature (or a bath) is refreshing, grounding, centering, and immune system boosting.

You can also do different meditative exercises to ground; such as breathing in Unconditional Love energy and grounding Earth energy and exhaling out all the energy you no longer need (in the form of smoke), then visualizing roots of energy coming from the Earth and going up your spine, chakras, and feet to send you healing and grounding energy nutrients. Always remember to thank Mother Nature, yourself, and the energy once this is complete.

Grounding should be done on a daily basis and whenever you are feeling lightheaded, uncentered, angry, resentful, anxious, depressed, fearful, or confused.

Grounding is the key to deep communication on multiple levels of experience. When you ground and center yourself, you become present with your surroundings and you can feel and experience the heartbeat within all life to a greater extent.

We will now cover ways to ground yourself more in-depth.

**Method 1- The Physical**

You can hug a tree, relax in a garden, be present with deep breaths while standing outside, go swimming, lay in water, eat nuts, drink water mindfully, stand outside (or walk outside) barefoot, lay on Mother Earth, do yoga, receive or give a massage, or do anything that brings you fully centered in the present moment. Mindfulness is key.

**Method 2- Energy Work**

Take deep breaths. I recommend inhaling for a count of 1-2-3-4, holding for 1-2-3-4-5, and releasing for 1-2-3-4-5-6. Repeat this breathing process 3-6 times. Once the deep breathing is complete, be present within your body. Do an internal scan to feel and experience yourself at this moment. Feel within from your head to your toes, noticing anything from positive tingling to pain. Put no thoughts to your experience, just feel and be present. Feel your feelings instead of thinking them.

Untense your muscles as you experience feeling throughout your body. If there is any tension, all you need to say is, "I release this tension and let go of all that does not serve me for the greatest and highest good. I accept and embrace understanding of the source of this tension. I am open to growth."

Once you have completed the body scan, bring your focus to your heart space- located in the center of your heart chakra (in the middle of your chest- the heart chakra is not where the blood heart is).

Say this out loud or in your mind: "I call upon and ask for grounding healing roots of energy to come from the heart of Mother Earth and connect to my chakras, my body, and my energy channel for divine grounding, protection, and healing all that needs to be released and transformed." You can speak this the way I shared it or you can feel free to intuitively choose your own ways of expressing the same intention. Either you can say this intention with your power and belief and then just relax and allow the energy to flow within you, or you can also visualize energetic roots coming from the heart of Mother Earth, spreading throughout your form, and centering you in the present moment. When I envision the roots, I visualize pink-flowing energy, brown earth tones, and green moss flowing within the roots. You can follow your intuition with what feels right.

Know that energy always knows intention. Visualization is optional and should be guided intuitively. Trust is the most valuable. Intention is manifestation. Intention is creation. Intention is permission.

### *Method 3: Frequency and Sound*

You can listen to a grounding frequency. This could include drumming, nature sounds, root chakra meditation music, etc. I typically search "root chakra music" or "grounding music" on Youtube's search bar and feel which one resonates. You can listen to this music while being present and allowing yourself to relax into the sounds frequency for around 10 minutes or until you feel grounded.

Frequency is incredible. 528 Hz is an excellent frequency for aiding in the process of communicating with animals and for increasing unconditional love. It is known as the *miracle tone*. You can find music on Youtube with this frequency by searching "528 Hz" in the search bar.

Singing bowls are also a wonderful way to ground yourself, as is singing.

Learn the Art of Channelin

There are many more ways to reconnect and center. You can intuitively follow and explore what resonates with you.

Love and connect on.

# Downloading Unconditional Love Energy

The energy of unconditional love is powerful, healing, protective, and transformative. Love awakens the good in all and brings harmony and balance universally. Love creates the most positively powerful of changes.

It is beneficial for you to send and call upon this love for yourself on a daily basis. It is also beneficial for you to call upon this love with the intention of it connecting to the core of each and every essence, being, and consciousness in this universe and beyond. Intention is manifestation. Intention is creation. This love can transform negative entities back to their core love-centered selves, help spirits find peace, spark empathy and compassion in others, and so much more.

Love heals all.

Everyone experiences energy differently. Many feel the energy in the form of warmth, tingling, coolness, or a light touch. Others may visually see the energy. Some hear or even smell the energy. Certain individuals may not physically notice the energy at all, and instead have an intuitive inner knowing of the energy's presence.

Typically over time, you will experience the energy stronger and stronger. Be patient, trust your intuition, and continue to practice and build a relationship with the consciousness and energy. They feel and know you completely.

There are 2 ways that I will show you in this class for connecting to Unconditional Love energy.

You can begin by setting your intention at the beginning of sending yourself Unconditional Love Energy for the energy to go to the root cause of your struggles. To do this you can say, "I set my intention for Unconditional Love energy to go towards the root cause of my struggles." You can change the wording and say it in any way that resonates with you. Intention is manifestation and creation.

I also recommend playing meditation music or nature sounds if this resonates with you.

**The first method for connecting with this energy is to download Unconditional Love.** Once the initial downloading process is complete, all you need to do is call upon the energy whenever you wish to heal with her.

To begin the downloading process, complete a grounding exercise. Once the grounding exercise is complete; close your eyes, sit or stand comfortably with your hands resting and your palms facing towards the sky.

Now, say this out loud or within your mind, "I call upon and ask for the purest and most powerful of Unconditional Love energy to download into one or both of my hands- wherever the energy resonates. I unconditionally love this energy and myself. I will only heal and connect with this energy with the intentions of the greatest and highest good of all. I am grateful for all this love does, is, and brings." Then just rest and relax. Allow the energy to fully integrate into your being. You may feel warmth, coolness, or a tingling sensation in one or both hands. Be open and trust the experience. Sometimes people may also see, hear, or smell the energy. Be open to any responses you may have.

After a minute or so, you can say this out loud or in your mind, "I call and ask for this Unconditional Love energy to enter the entirety of my being and resonate wherever is best for the greatest and highest good. This energy is also downloading within my heart chakra and heart space if it is for the greatest and highest good. I relax and go with the flow of love." Just relax for a few minutes, be present, and allow for the energy to fully merge with your being.

After the initial completion, all you need to do to call upon and connect with this energy is to put out your hands (with the palms facing toward the sky) and say this out loud or within your mind, "I call upon the purest of Unconditional Love energy at this time with the intention of the greatest and highest good".

After you call upon the energy, you can send the love to yourself. To do this just say, "Unconditional Love energy is flowing continuously towards and within myself for the greatest and highest good. The energy will slowly cease once the embrace and awakening are complete." You may feel, sense, or experience the energy in different ways. Your hands can hover above your body- although I typically rest my hands on my heart chakra or on a place that needs assistance. This is entirely up to you. I typically feel the energy the strongest when my hands are either resting on my heart chakra or hovering above.

Remember; intention is manifestation. When you intend to receive Unconditional Love energy, then you will.

**The second method for healing and connecting with Unconditional Love energy is through the breath.** To begin this process, set your intention. I recommend saying, "I set my intention to breathe in pure love energy with every inhale and release pure love energy with every exhale. With every inhale, this energy will flow into my being for healing what is needed for the greatest and highest good. With every exhale, I will release love into life and all."

Either you can just set this intention and then focus on your breathing for around 5-30 minutes- until you feel the energy is complete- or you can visualize this powerful love energy being inhaled and exhaled within your form.

I highly encourage thanking the energy, yourself, and Mother Earth at the end of every love-energy connection to provide deeper connection through gratitude and appreciation. You can also drink some fresh juice, tea, or water and take a few deep and mindful breaths.

# Activating and Maintaining a Merkaba Field

A Merkaba field is meant to surround your being in the shape of a high-frequency star tetrahedron. The Merkaba field balances divine feminine and masculine energy with Earth and Starlight.

This field assists in protection, connection, divine communication, inner awakening, ability learning, expanding, and much more.

You can establish this energy field for yourself and children under the age of 6. Once this energy field is established, it is beneficial to send Unconditional Love energy and gratitude to your Merkaba to form a strong relationship, connection, understanding, and increase the strength and ability of this field. Forming a friendship and strong communication with your Merkaba is also beneficial for achieving specific goals.

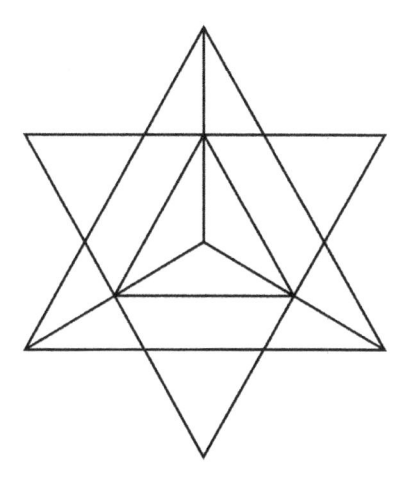

A Merkaba will follow your intention and can be set to follow your desired positive manifestation wishes. Your soul's intentions, trust systems, and understandings greatly influence your Merkaba field.

Merkabas are always connected to source energy and have access to unlimited positive possibilities.

You can begin the process of activation by grounding yourself, relaxing, and sending yourself Unconditional Love Energy.

Once the preparation process is complete, close your eyes and picture the star tetrahedrons surrounding your being. The divine masculine aspect points upwards and spins clockwise. This will begin at your knees and extend several feet above your head.

The divine female aspect points downwards, beginning at your shoulders and extending several feet below your feet. This aspect will be spinning counterclockwise.

Breathe in and out slowly and fully with the intention of connecting your breath to the prana and unconditional love that is increasing to form and bind into the Merkaba field.

It is recommended to say, "I connect with, breathe with, and embrace the prana and unconditional love that is increasing and expanding to form and create this Merkaba field that is surrounding me and becoming a part of me."

Embrace the power, protection, love, and ability that is forming around you and surrounding you. Embrace the unlimited, beautiful, peaceful, positive, and loving Merkaba. Relax and just be.
Set your intentions as to how the Merkaba will operate (you can always add more specific intentions later). I recommend saying, "This Merkaba field has a foundation of unconditional love, prana, light, and peace. This field only operates for the greatest and highest good of all with the most loving of intentions. I call for and ask this Merkaba to protect me continuously, heal me, work with me to spread love and fulfill my mission, and assist in providing peace, continuous positive growth, and positive abundance. I feel strong and beautiful unconditional loving gratitude for this

Merkaba, for myself, and for all. And so it is."

At this time you can rest, relax, and feel your Merkaba. You can also send this Merkaba Unconditional Love Energy, light, and gratitude daily or whenever you feel intuitively drawn to do so. This field is a part of you and is your friend. It is important for you to trust and embrace this field and yourself as you are now continuously connected. You can even have various conversations and communicate in many ways to strengthen this bond and increase positive power, ability, and focused intention.

To form a Merkaba field around young children, it is the same process (which you can say and visualize on their behalf), but should be done when they are resting or sleeping with the visualization and intention of unconditional love around them. You can explain to them that they have a field of protection and positive love surrounding them that is their friend and guide. You can tell them that they can communicate with their Merkaba friend and always ask their Merkaba field for help, assistance, and love.

Once established, a Merkaba field shall always reside with you for the rest of your lifetime and potentially beyond this lifetime.

# Raising Your Vibration

Everything and everyone has a vibration. This vibration can either be high and balanced or low, unhealed, and fear-based.

The lowest vibrational things to consume and use are the bodies and byproducts of the dead and sentient lives who have suffered (this includes fur, meat, dairy, silk, commercial honey, and eggs), alcohol, highly processed and modified foods, and man-made drugs.

Having a clean plant-based diet is extremely important. Eating the murdered bodies of animals who have lived their entire lives enslaved by humans will not help you connect to love, and will certainly lower your vibrational frequency. 99.9% of the animals farmed in the USA come from factory farms. The other .1% do not live the happy, joyful, and free lives that are marketed to us.

Dairy can cause high levels of inflammation and is meant for a baby cow, not the adults of another species. Calves are either killed at birth if they are boys or taken away and kept in little cages if they are girls. The girls are given formula and are not allowed to drink milk from their mothers. It is a cruel process. Once a mother is artificially inseminated a few times, she will be killed for cheap meat. The dairy industry is the meat industry.

Millions of baby boy chicks are killed every year because the egg industry views them as useless as they cannot produce eggs. They are killed within a few hours to a few days of being born (these babies are typically ground up alive). The female chicks are deprived of their mothers and are typically debeaked- which is a very painful process. Chickens have been bred to produce over 30 times the amount of eggs their bodies originally produced by nature. They are killed and eaten or disposed of as soon as their egg production declines.

Virtually all farmed fish live in factory farm conditions. Trillions of innocent fish are brutally murdered yearly for our pallet. The nets used for commercial fishing cause the death of millions besides their intended victims- including whales and dolphins. These nets also create large amounts of pollution. It has been proven that fish feel pain. Unfortunately, it is predicted that we may have fishless oceans by 2050 if we don't stop this needless massacre.

Eating abuse and violence is traumatic for the body, mind, soul, and spirit. It increases apathy, illness, fear, and disconnection. Eating fear creates fear.

For the same reason that you cannot love someone and abuse them is why you cannot love animals and eat them. Paying for exploitation and murder is not love.

I know it can be hard to change your lifestyle, but the lives of so many depend on it. Each day living compassionately, you can save the life of 1 animal (or more), 1,100 gallons of water, 40 pounds of grain, 30 sq ft of forest, and 20 lbs of CO2.[1] Animal agriculture is a leading cause of biodiversity loss, water and air pollution, and deforestation.[2]

---

[1] Mantilla, Stephanie. "Vegan Calculator: What's the Environmental Impact of Going Vegan?" *Plant Prosperous*, 29 Nov. 2021,
https://plantprosperous.com/vegan-calculator/#:~:text=So%2C%20how%20much%20do%20vegans,a%20vegan%20saves%20the%20equivalent.

[2] "Animal Agriculture's Impact on Climate Change." *Climate Nexus*, 13 Nov. 2019,https://climatenexus.org/climate-issues/food/animal-agricultures-impact-on-climate-change/#:~:text=Anima

Changing the world starts with the choices you make daily; the clothes you wear, the food you eat, the way you treat others and yourself, the thoughts you think, and the actions you take.

I am here to assist in this journey of compassionate living. If you would like to have a free mentor to assist in this transition then please email me at chloe@magentasunhealing.com. Eating plant-based is affordable, simple, healthy, uplifting, healing, and balanced if you do it in an aligned way. Anyone can transition. There is always a way to live compassionately no matter the circumstances. I am here to assist you on this journey.

It's essential to choose a life of non-violence and peace. The more peace and love you emit, the more love and positive abundance you and others shall receive in return.

---

l%20agriculture%20is%20the%20second,air%20pollutio n%20and%20biodiversity%20loss.

## **Here is a list of what you can do to raise your vibration naturally**

1. Eat fruit and drink coconut water/fresh juice.

2. Eat an animal and animal-product-free diet.

3. Eliminate alcohol.

4. Stay clear from heavily processed, fried, GMO's, and heavily pesticide-sprayed food.

5. Practice safe sun-gazing.

6. Reading/meditating/dancing/fulfilling your passions instead of scrolling through social media or watching T.V.

7. Reducing fear-based emotions through mindfulness and reawakening love.

8. Embracing why you are here and pursuing your life's mission.

9. Hugs/cuddles/physical affection.

10. Share kind and loving words and affirmations.

11. Spending time in nature.

12. Practice deep and full breaths.

13. Laugh and smile.

14. Embrace all of life from the highs to the lows to the mediums.

15. Let go of the past and try your best to embrace change.

16. Follow your intuition and embrace your highest self.

17. Love yourself and all life with all of your being.

18. Hug and love yourself.

19. Spread and share gratitude for all of life from the challenging to the uplifting aspects.

20. Connect to natural bodies of water.

21. Dream and hope.

22. Listen to positive frequencies and uplifting music, and ask your body to match the vibration that resonates with embracing your highest and most love-centered self.

# Various Positive Beings, Essences, and Consciousnesses

There are many beings, essences, and consciousnesses that you have the ability to connect with and channel.

Some include; angels, higherselves, spirit guides, balanced spirits, animal essences, flower essences (like blue lotus flowers), herbal essences, energy essences, unconditional love conciousness, water consciousness, and Mother Earth consciousness. You can also channel positive beings from other dimensions and/or planets such as Pleidians, Arcturians, Yahyell, Fendorians, and many more.

As long as you set your intentions to only connect with beings, essences, and consciousnesses that are beneficial for the greatest and highest good then you will only connect to positive and/or neutral individuals. Know that you always have the opportunity and ability to disconnect from who you are channeling at any moment. You are safe and protected. You can also call upon angels for assistance at any time.

The more you can let go while surrendering to love, the better. Follow your intuition with who you wish to channel and connect with. The possibilities are endless. You can even stick to channeling solely source love or your higher self if you choose.

# Surrender and Trust

Surrendering to love is essential while learning how to trust yourself, trust the one you are channeling, trust love, and always trust that you are protected. If you lack trust, you may be leaning into fear.

Being aware is important. Trust does not imply blindness. Your intuition should be strong and present to lead you to the awareness of what resonates and feels right and what doesn't.

It is common for people to confuse surrender and trust with being naive but this couldn't be farther from the truth. Surrendering to love and trusting the universe boosts your intuition, provides miracles and synchronicities, and assists you on your path.

It is also important to learn how to replace your instinct with intuition. Instinct is based on past experiences whether this may be from past lives, ancestral, or current life circumstances. Instinct is fear-based and focused on survival. Because instinct is only based on the past, it cannot be used to fully evolve on the path moving forward and can be inaccurate with new situations that may arise. For instance, a scary-looking being may not be negative at all even though their form may look uncomfortable to us. In contrast, a beautiful-looking being could be very dangerous. We need to be able to tap into our intuition to find the truth instead of using past experiences to dictate how to move forward. Being guided by fear is never the answer.

Certain aspects of instinct are sometimes beneficial but any beneficial aspect of instinct is already found in intuition.

Intuition is guided by source love, the universe, your higher self, and spirit guides. It is always new and changing based on what is needed in the current moment. It feels calm, balanced, real, and connected. It flows and never connects to stress. It feels like a loving pull. Intuition can provide you with guidance, and knowledge, and leads to discovering luminosity and synchronicities.

Whenever you feel something come up, ask yourself what you are feeling. This can help to determine whether instinct or intuition is guiding you. Also, try practicing mindfulness exercising with the intention of replacing instinct with intuition. It takes time and awareness. Ask yourself questions and find the root of what is happening.

Surrendering to love while trusting in the universe naturally boosts intuition.

You can also look up on Youtube, "binaural beats for boosting and connecting to intuition" to assist.

# What Does Channeling Feel Like?

Honestly, it can range drastically from person to person. For some, it may feel like they are being gently guided. For others, it may feel like they are deep underground in a cool but pressurized cave. There are also people who report feeling like they are in a deep sleep or relaxed trance. Others may feel as though they are floating and hovering above their body looking below.

For me personally, it feels different depending on who I am channeling, the method I used for connection, and how I am feeling that day.

It ranges from me feeling like I am inside or a part of rock deep underground with an intense vibrating pressure that also feels calming and energizing to feeling an intense buzzing pressure in my third eye with a fiery sensation that feels very alive. Many times, I just experience a very calm and relaxed feeling while I just sit in the corner of my own mind, being a gentle observer of what the channeled being is experiencing.

If I am having a day where I am feeling very sad or in need of assistance, the being I channel will typically begin by guiding me into an energy healing chamber or space to recharge and heal before temporarily occupying my body.

For me, it feels very uplifting, comforting, and re-energizing to channel. It feels like a much-needed reset to give my mind a break from being in charge all the time. I love feeling the incredible energies of whose who I channel as well. Their wisdom, awareness, love, and feeling are incredible and inspiring.

Be open to your own personal experiences. Everyone is different and every time is unique. Release expectations and just be.

# Different Forms of Channel Expression

You are able to channel write, channel speak, channel heal, channel feel, channel create, and channel move. Each is unique, beautiful, and just what it needs to be. Always focus on being open to whichever expression feels right and allow for the being to guide.

Channel writing is connecting to a being, essence, or consciousness in order to physically write anything from words, to numbers, to images and drawings. This is typically done quietly and could go on from a few minutes to a few hours. You may even write in a different language other than the ones you consciously know. If you choose this method of connection, it is important to really let go and allow for your hand to glide. There is no need to use your analytical mind during channeling. Save the analytical mind for later and just be present and open.

I have written entire books channeling various beings from animals to Unconditional Love Consciousness for Unconditional Love Reiki. I have also channeled my higher self in various writings including my first ever book. I would say that channel writing is my common preference as I feel it is very easy for me to relax into it for long periods of time.

Channel speaking is allowing the channeled individual to use your vocal cords to express through you. This could come in the form of light languages, various healing sounds and noises, singing, and human language like the ones you typically speak. This is one of the most common forms of channeling and can be beneficial for providing sessions for people where questions are answered or for providing verbal wisdom and healing to the masses.

Channel healing is the ability and art of channeling a being, consciousness, energy, or essence through you in order to provide either self-healing or healing outwards for all or another individual. I have provided channeled healing sessions by embracing the consciousnesses, souls, and spirits of various beings; such as Arcturians, Pleiadians, and Angels. These healing sessions vary in the way they are experienced and presented, both from my own perspective and the receiver's perspective. These healing sessions can be incredibly powerful and intense as healing methods from various dimensions, planes, and places are channeled for incredible results. Every being heals in their own way so no 2 sessions are the same.

Channel feeling is merging with a being, consciousness, energy, and/or essence, and feeling with them. You could even channel yourself within another to feel how it is to be them and to experience what is beneficial to be shared. This can help to gain greater understanding, compassion, empathy, growth, and wisdom. It can be incredibly heart and mind-opening as well. Some of my most transformative experiences have come from channeling my awareness into another- often times my Higher Self or various natural animal individuals.

Channel creating can include channeling an energy, consciousness, essence, and/or being to create art, imagery, machinery, technology, inventions, modalities of healing, and so much more. There are many visionaries who channel on this Earth and many other places to introduce already existing ideas into new life in a new place.

Channel movement is channeling an energy, consciousness, essence, and/or being to dance, provide energy healing, various physical poses, or even walk with your body. This can feel very unique and freeing. On occasion, I channel a being who will go for a walk outside or feel various surroundings and this always feels very special because of the way they are very mindfully and purposefully being present in life. I feel beautiful life force flowing throughout my being when this happens. They may also introduce various stretches or methods of movement for you or others that can offer many benefits. I have channeled beings to demonstrate how to gather pranic energy using movement before as well.

Channeling is not limited to one method or experience. It can be experienced and flow differently for different individuals. Trying your best to be open to various possibilities and to trust in source is the most valuable. You are doing beautifully awakening your heart and opening your love for incredible changes.

# Cleansing Your Channel

Cleansing and opening up your channel with source love and bright light is important to increase your ability to channel fully and clearly.

This can be done before every channeling, daily, or whenever you feel you are experiencing blockages and/or fear.

To begin, allow yourself to rest comfortably by laying or sitting down with your palms facing the sky.

Breathe in for a count of 1. 2. 3. 4. Hold for 1. 2. 3. 4. 5. Exhale for a count of 1. 2. 3. 4. 5. 6. Repeat this breathing 3-5 times or however long resonates with you.

Once completed, allow your breathing to rest slightly deeper than it usually is for you and make sure you exhale and inhale fully.

Now, share a few words of gratitude and pure genuine love in any way that resonates you, with source love and all founded from and on source love- including yourself, your higher self, and your spirit guides.

After this is complete, make sure your spine is aligned and as straight as it is able to be in this current moment and say the following words out loud or within your heart mind, "I call upon and ask for the brightest and purest of light and the most genuine of source love to connect within and around me with the intention of opening up my energy channel through my chakras and meridian points for the greatest and highest good. I let go and open myself up to receiving this cleansing energy and letting go- allowing all that is not for the greatest and highest good to transform into love."

Now, take a few deep breaths and just relax. Allow yourself to let go and truly be present. You may experience various sensations, images, thoughts, and feelings- just be with them and be with yourself.

If you feel guided to, you can also visualize this bright light and source love cleansing your channel and connecting with your being. This is option to you.

Allow yourself to rest with the energy for as long as you feel guided to. This could be from anywhere from 5 minutes to hours.

Once completed, share a few more feelings and words of gratitude and genuine love with source love and light and take a few more deep inhales and exhales, setting your intention moving forward to embrace the most loving of journeys and awakenings.

# Entering the Heart Space Method of Connection/ Channeling

The heart space is located within the center of the heart chakra. It is a wonderful space that can be connected to for meditation, manifestation, animal communication, past-life viewing, trauma healing, distance energy sessions, channeling, communication with higher selves, spirits, spirit guides, beings, consciousnesses, essences, and more.

I highly recommend beginning your connections and/or channeling by setting the intention to connect with animal individuals, Mother Nature Consciousness, your spirit guides, your higher self, Unconditional Love Consciousness, and angels within this space. These are all wonderful and uplifting beings to connect with.

The heart space can either be designed by you or it can be designed by the individual you are connecting with -as in, the theme and feel of the space. I typically set my intention that the heart space will appear in any way that resonates for the greatest and highest good. Typically, I experience various colors and frequencies of energy vibrating, sometimes nature, crystal caves, bodies of water, bright light, and more. This varies for every connection.

Some people only experience color in the heart space. This could be flowing pink, gentle blue, earth green, or another color. This color typically has symbolism and always has meaning. It is very powerful for the healing process when experienced. The color I most commonly view is a swirling mixture of pink and green- Unconditional Love with Earth grounding.

Some people may not visually see anything at all within this space. Instead, they may solely feel or hear within the space. This is also very natural. Everyone may connect with their senses in different ways and every way is just as effective. You may go into the heart space and feel what the being is currently feeling or what they have felt in the past (or even the future). You may hear their responses in the form of words, visuals, sounds (like whistling or a high-pitched frequency), thoughts, or a voice.

Every connection you experience is valuable.

To begin the process of connecting within the heart space, ground yourself. Grounding is incredibly important as it allows your mind to rest and be present. It also helps in balancing your chakras and connecting you with animal individuals and Mother Earth.

After you have grounded yourself, you can set your intention. An example of this intention is to say, "I set my intention to go within my heart space and consciously connect with the mind, body, soul, spirit, and emotions of this being (or other if you are connecting with an essence or consciousness) for the greatest and highest good. I am open to accepting anything beneficial to understand and receive from this being. I set my intention that I will bring my conscious awareness down to my heart space, then open the door to my heart space to reveal a wonderful place that resonates for the greatest and highest good. If beneficial, I will channel this being in harmony. Once our connection is complete, we will both be grounded back in the present moment within our head and heart minds. I call upon my higher self, my spirit guides, Unconditional Love consciousness, and Mother Earth to send protection, love, guidance, support, and anything else that is beneficial for our greatest and highest good."

Next, you can play music if this resonates with you. I recommend listening to a frequency such as 528 Hz or nature sounds which can be found on Youtube. Then, close your eyes and bring your focus and attention to your breath. Breathe in for a count of 1-2-3-4, hold for 1-2-3-4-5, and let go for 1-2-3-4-5-6. Repeat this deep and mindful breathing a minimum of 3 times. Truly feel and experience your breath from within. Experience your life with all of your being. After you finish with the deep breathing, you can allow your breathing to flow back to normal or slightly deeper than normal.

Now, bring your focus and attention inwards. If you're a visual person, you can visualize a staircase being created in any design that resonates with you, leading from your headspace to your heart space (in the center of your chest- where your heart chakra is located). If you are more feeling-based, you can bring your feeling, focus, and attention inwards. In the same way you are able to feel your right hand, your left foot, or feel when your nose is cold or being lightly touched, you can also bring your attention to other places- such as your heart space. If you prefer verbal intention, you can say this out loud or in your mind, "I am now descending downwards to reach my heart space in my heart chakra."

Once you reach the entrance to your heart space, you can either visually see yourself opening a door and entering this space, you can feel the love within this space, or you can say, "I am now entering my heart space." (All 3 are also good to do together if you would like to engage with multiple senses.)

Within this space you may notice some feelings or see some visuals, a smell or a new feeling may connect with you, or a voice may be heard. Notice and explore your surroundings. Trust your intuition with this. If it just seems like a dark space then create a light. Know that you have full creative positive freedom within this space.

The heart space does not allow fear-based energy to enter. Sometimes there may be experiences of grief, sadness, or pain (depending on how you are feeling consciously and subconsciously and what is being shown to you to experience), but it is always a safe space to be in. A negative entity is unable to enter this space for any reason.

Once you are settled within this heart space, you can call upon the being, essence, or consciousness of your choosing by saying, "I now invite ... to enter this space and connect with me if it is for the greatest and highest good." If you are not connecting with a specific being and you wish to see who wants to reach out to you, then you can say, "I invite in any positive and love-centered being, consciousness, energy, or essence who has a message to share or a connection to be made at this time." Know that by using any communication method, you are able to connect to beings in dense/physical form or spirit.

Once the being is invited into the space, you can patiently wait for them to connect with you. They may appear instantaneously or it may take some time. You may be able to visually see them and even interact with them, or it could be a more feeling or verbal interaction. You can ask them questions (even if you do not notice them in the space yet) and patiently be open to the response.

*Sometimes a response may come in the form of a thought.* It is very important to trust this thought. The being may show you a picture perspective or a video visual as a response, give you a feeling either emotionally or physically, or respond verbally.

It is important not to talk over the individual as this can create missed communication. Think of when you are talking to a person on the phone. If you are thinking about your next response or what their next response could be while they are talking or silent, you could miss important information that could be said. Being patient and an active listener is very important. Let go of your analytical mind and embrace your present and intuitive mind.

Within this space, you can share messages, feelings, pictures, and ideas while receiving information. Be open to anything that comes. The experiences will change and grow with every connection.

If you would like to channel this being, essence, energy, or consciousness, you can do so at this time. To begin, set your intentions by saying this out loud or in your mind, "At this time I invite this being to channel through my chakras and being if it is for the greatest and highest good. I allow myself to rest within the heart space as I am being channeled through and I surrender to source love."

The most important thing for you to do is to trust and relax. If at any time you would like to stop channeling, all you need to do is say, "at this time I will no longer channel this being. I ask for them to reside back within my heart space to allow this channeling connection to conclude for the time being. I love and appreciate their energy spent connecting with me in this way." Remember; your intention is your manifestation.

Channeling is a different experience for each individual. Let go and allow for the being to guide your body and mind. You can always think of the experience later. Now is the time to just be.

Once this connection through communication and/or channeling feels complete (typically anywhere between 2 minutes- 3 hours), you can kindly ask for the individual to leave your heart space or they may leave on their own. It is important to thank them for their connection. I would suggest saying something similar to, "Thank you for your connection, all you are, and all you will be. I greatly appreciate you and I unconditionally love you. I ask for you to release from my heart space at this time. Thank you for all that you are and all you continue to be."

You can complete the session by slowly bringing your consciousness and awareness back to your headspace. Sometimes people also enjoy visually going back up the stairs.

You can then wiggle your fingers and your toes and take a few deep inhales and slow exhales. The session is completed when you share gratitude with Mother Earth and all the energies and beings who helped with this connection ( including yourself). You can drink some water or juice and write down your experiences. Writing is beneficial as sometimes you can forget the information you receive in meditation. It is common to forget channelings either immediately or after a few minutes. You will remember something if you are meant to.

You can practice this exercise whenever you feel called to do so. I recommend practicing connection daily or at least a few times a week. Any language, skill, or learning can take time and practice to master. Take your time and allow the process to naturally continue, flow, and your connections to expand.

You are safe and everything aligns in divine timing.

If this method doesn't resonate with you, it is possible that another method will connect with you more. Be open to what feels right and follow your intuition.

# Entering the Heart Portal Method of Connection/ Channeling

I discovered this form of communication (consciously) in the Spring of 2021. In one meditation, Mother Nature's consciousness shared how to connect and communicate through this method.

I love connecting to animal individuals, Mother Earth consciousness, Unconditional Love consciousness, and my higher self especially with this method- although it can be used to connect with any being, energy, essence, or consciousness. This is the method I connect with the most frequently at this time (in 2022). It feels very grounding, centering, and love-awakening from my perspective and resonates quite deeply.

To begin this method of connection, ground yourself in the way or ways that resonate most with you.

Set your intentions for healing, communication, deep connection, awakening love, and channeling if it is beneficial. You can say, "I set my intention for healing, communication, deep connection, awakening love, and channeling this being if it is beneficial for the greatest and highest good. I ask for Mother Earth's consciousness, my spirit guides, my higher self, and Unconditional Love consciousness to bless and awaken this connection. I am grateful for all and love all, including myself."

Allow yourself to rest comfortably either laying or sitting, then bring your attention and focus to your breathing. Breathe in for a count of 1-2-3-4, hold for 1-2-3-4-5, and release for 1-2-3-4-5-6. Repeat this breathing process 3 times or as many times as you feel is needed for yourself, then allow your breathing to rest back to normal or slightly deeper than normal.

Call upon unconditional love energy in your heart chakra and your hands. You can say, "I call upon the purest and brightest of Unconditional Love energy to grow and expand within my heart chakra and flow from my hands. I ask for this energy to create a universal bridge of connection for this being and myself, for the strongest of communication and understanding of one another."

Now, bring your hands and rest them on your heart chakra and allow your focus and attention to be within the center of your chest, where your heart chakra resides.

Invite the being, energy, essence, or consciousness to connect with you at this time. This can be said out loud or within your mind by saying, "I invite in this being for communication, loving connection, and channeling at this time if it is meant to be."

Be patient and open for this connection. You can speak towards this being, send them Unconditional Love energy, and receive information in the form of words, visions, feelings, and more.

To send them unconditional love energy, you can say, "I call upon the most powerful and loving of unconditional love energy to be sent to this being for the greatest and highest good. I ask for them to be open to receiving and accepting this energy if it is for the greatest and highest good."

Follow your intuition. Allow communication to naturally flow. Take your time. Trust yourself and the one you are connecting with. You are doing wonderfully.

If you feel a pull to channel, then you can do so at this time. To begin, set your intention by saying this out loud or in your mind, "At this time I invite this being to channel through my chakras and being if it is for the greatest and highest good. I allow myself to rest within the heart portal in my heart chakra and be intuitively guided as I am being channeled through. I surrender to source love."

The most important thing is for you to trust and relax. If at any time you would like to stop channeling, all you need to do is say, "at this time I will no longer channel this being. I ask for them to reside back within my heart chakra to allow this channeling connection to conclude for the time being. I love and appreciate their energy spent connecting with me in this way." Remember; your intention is your manifestation.

Channeling is a different experience for every individual. Let go and allow for the being to guide your body and mind. You can always think of the experience later. Now is the time to just be.

Take your time and allow for all to flow in balance.

Whenever you feel the connection is complete, you can say out loud or in your mind, "Thank you source love, light, and all positive beings and energies for supporting this divine connection. Thank you being for all that you are. I unconditionally love you and I wish you the absolute best. We will connect again if it is meant to be." This signifies the completion of this connection. Your intention for disconnection is your manifestation.

Once completed, you can bring your attention back to your headspace whenever you're ready, take deep breaths, relax, and recenter yourself.

Remember, you are naturally a being of love.

# Above the Crown Method of Connection/ Channeling

This method of connection is wonderful especially if you are feeling stuck, heavy, or fatigued within your body- but it really requires strong and secure grounding beforehand. Otherwise, you may feel a bit lightheaded or uneasy. This method is wonderful for people who prefer bringing their attention above and out of their body, experiencing more in spirit, than within their body- experiencing more in soul.

With this method in particular, I find that people either love connecting with this method or that it doesn't resonate with them at all. Let go and experience what feels right for you. This method is safe and you are safe to try it.

To begin, provide yourself with a grounding exercise, energy, and/or experience of your choosing. Once this is completed, then you can begin some deep and slow breathing with the intention of being present.

This exercise is typically more visual-based but it can be done through strictly feeling and other senses if this resonates more with you.

Breathe in for a count of 1-2-3-4.
Hold for a count of 1-2-3-4-5.
Let go for a count of 1-2-3-4-5-6.
*Repeat this 3 times or more if you feel intuitively guided to do so.*

At this time, you can allow your breathing to go back to usual or slightly deeper and you can visualize a small version of yourself in your mind. This version of you will have wings or some sort of floatation device; such as a flying carpet, jet-pack or just having the ability to float. If you are more of a feeling or verbal connector, then at this time you can focus on the feeling of being able to fly and float and say these words out loud or within your heart mind, "At this time I connect with my spirit self and allow myself to begin flying upwards, transcending my physical form and rising through my crown chakra and above my being. I am safe, loved, and connected."

Allow yourself to start floating or flying upward until you are above your head (which can be visualized or just felt and trusted. The same way you can bring your attention to your hand, foot, heart, or head is the same way that you can bring your attention right outside of your body).

When you reach above, you can visualize yourself being in the clouds, sitting on a treetop, or even being amongst the stars, or you can just feel yourself above and say, "I am now above my crown." Then you can say, "I ask source love for assistance in connecting and communicating with this being at this time. I relax and invite this being to share this experience with me."

Take your time and be open to this being, consciousness, energy, or essence connecting with you. You may see, feel, hear, or even smell them. Be open in the ways they are presented and experienced by you. Each experience and every connection is unique. You can ask questions, share feelings and thoughts, share gratitude and love, and anything else that resonates. Any way you experience them is beautiful.

Just relax and allow any experiences to come to you. Try not to force anything, just relax and trust. Surrender into love and the present moment.

If you feel a pull to channel, then you can do so at this time. To begin, set your intentions by saying this out loud or in your mind, "At this time I invite this being to channel through my chakras and being if it is for the greatest and highest good. I allow myself to rest above my crown chakra and just be present, absorbing, feeling, and exploring anything that is meant to be experienced. I surrender to source love and let go of control."

The most important thing for you to do is to trust and relax. If at any time you would like to stop channeling, all you need to do is say, "at this time I will no longer channel this being. I ask for them to reside back above my crown to allow this channeling connection to conclude for the time being. I love and appreciate their energy spent connecting with me in this way."

Remember; your intention is your manifestation. Channeling is a different experience for each individual. Let go and allow for the being to guide your body and mind. You can always think of the experience later. Now is the time to just be.

Now, just follow your intuition and embrace the present love-based experience.

Whenever you feel ready, you can begin to start floating or flying down until you are back resting in your body. This can be done by visuals (imagination), feeling, or solely by verbal intention and acknowledgment. Breathe in for a count of 1-2-3-4, hold for 1-2-3-4-5, and let go for 1-2-3-4-5-6.

You can open your eyes whenever you feel ready. Drink some water and eat some fruit or raw nuts- such as cashews- or ground yourself using any method of your choosing.

Love on <3

# Beside You Method of Connection/ Channeling

This method of connection is typically used for mediumship (communication with spirits) but can be connected to for channeling as well. The biggest difference for this method is that you are connecting to whoever or whatever is currently around you. You can still direct your intention on who you would like to connect with but it may be a bit more limited.

I rarely use this method of connection except if I am feeling someone around and wish to tap in to experience who or what is there.

It is up to you whether or not you would like to tune in and practice this method. It resonates for some but not all.

You can even begin by asking yourself, "does connecting with this method resonate with me?"

If it does then we can begin.

To start, ground yourself using any method or experience of your choosing. Once this is complete, take several slow and deep inhales and exhales.

Breathe in for a count of 1-2-3-4. Hold for 1-2-3-4-5. Exhale for a count of 1-2-3-4-5-6. Repeat this breathing process 3 times or as many times as it resonates with you.

Once completed, allow your breathing to rest at a slow and deep pace while setting your intention that with every inhale, you will breathe in pure love and bright light and with every exhale this love and light will be merging with your being and transforming all fear into love. This can be said with, "with every inhale, I am breathing in pure love and bright light, and with every exhale this love and light is merging with the entirety of my being while transforming all fear and blockages into divine pure love."

Now you can bring your attention and focus right outside of your body. In the same way you can have your attention and focus on any aspect of your body, like your hand, heart, or eyes, you can also have your attention and focus outside of your body to feel the energy, spirits, and beings that surround you. This can take some practice and time but intention is manifestation and it will become easier in divine timing if it feels challenging at first.

You can say this out loud or within your mind, "At this time, I invite communication with a positive being, energy, consciousness, essence, or spirit that is around me in this moment. I ask for this connection to be rooted in love and be beneficial for both of us for the greatest and highest good."

Take your time and feel around. You can ask questions, you can call upon unconditional love energy and share this energy with both of you, you can share words of gratitude or love, share experiences, and anything else that resonates with you.

It is possible that you may experience a combination of feeling, seeing, hearing, smelling, and more. Be open to whatever feels right. You may even be guided to connect with the *above the crown method* to further your communication.

If you feel a pull to channel, then you can do so at this time, if not, you can either continue the connection you have already begun or ask to be disconnected at this time and ground back in your body.

If you decide to channel with this method, bring your attention and focus to rest within your heart chakra during it.

To begin channeling, set your intentions by saying this out loud or in your mind, "At this time I invite this being to channel through my chakras and being if it is for the greatest and highest good. I allow myself to rest inside my heart chakra and just be present, absorbing, feeling, and exploring anything that is meant to be experienced. I surrender to source love and let go of control."

The most important thing is for you to trust and relax. If at any time you would like to stop channeling, all you need to do is say, "at this time I will no longer channel this being. I ask for them to reside back outside of my being to allow this channeling connection to conclude for the time being. I love and appreciate their energy spent connecting with me in this way."

Remember; your intention is your manifestation. Channeling is a different experience for each individual. Let go and allow for the being to guide your body and mind. You can always think of the experience later. Now is the time to just be.

Whenever complete, share a few more words and feelings of gratitude and love with the one you channeled and with source love as a whole and then just ground yourself, take some deep breaths, be present, and relax. You are doing beautifully and you are safe and loved.

# Within Another Method of Connection/ Channeling

This method is for connecting if you feel a pull and call to channel within someone instead of being channeled in.

For instance, sometimes if I am working with an animal individual who is suffering, I will channel into their being to feel what they are going through briefly to better assess how to move forward and to share with their loved ones what is happening from a first-hand perspective.

In addition to this, being able to channel into the form of a high vibrational and love-centered being, consciousness, energy, or essence can be quite transformative. This can be done by merging with them. I have channeled through and merged with my higher self before which opened my heart and all my chakras to the potential of life, full and true awakening, and the extent of my life's mission.

There are many reasons why doing this is beneficial and can lead to many positive results. It is safe to do and you will always come back to your being and form.

It is up to you on when, why, and how you choose to do this or even if you choose to do so at all. I don't do this all the time, only when I feel called to.

To begin connecting in this way, ground yourself in the method or experience of your choosing.

Once this is completed, take full and deep breaths. Know that you are safe. Stay present with life in the current everchanging moment.

Breathe in for a count of 1-2-3-4. Hold for 1-2-3-4-5. Let go for a count of 1-2-3-4-5-6. Repeat this breathing process 3 times or as many times as it resonates with you.

Once completed, allow your breathing to go back to normal or slightly deeper than how it normally resides for you.

Allow your focus to rest within your heart chakra and call upon pure unconditional love at this time to surround you, connect you with source love, and guide you moving forward. You can say this out loud or within your heart mind, "I call upon pure Unconditional Love Energy to surround me, connect me with source love, and guide me moving forward. I am open to embracing and surrendering to this love."

Relax and spend a few minutes just resting with and embracing this love energy.

When you feel ready to move forward, set your intention on who you intend to channel through. This can be done by saying, "I set my intention and ask to channel through this being if it is meant to happen and be accepted for the greatest and highest good. If not, I will not be able to channel through them and will be intuitively directed somewhere else where I am meant to be. I connect and embrace pure love and open my heart to follow what resonates with us both for the greatest and highest good."

Now, allow for your eyes to close and be truly present within your heart chakra and/or heart space. Have your attention and focus within the center of your chest, listening and experiencing through your heart mind.

Whenever you feel ready; visualize, feel, and/or call for a cord of energy to connect your heart chakra and third eye to the channel of the one you intend to channel through. If you wish to call upon the cord using words, you can say, "I call upon and ask for a cord of love-centered energy to connect my heart chakra and third eye to the channel of this individual if it is for the greatest and highest good." Relax and allow for the cord to be created.

Whenever you feel ready and a pull to do so, allow your spirit to lean outwards and travel through this cord into the intended being. This can be experienced through visuals, feelings, sounds, and/or words. Allow for the experience and intention to be guided by your intuition. Every experience is unique.

Once you are in the being of another, be present. Experience what it is like to be them and flow with their form. You can send them pure love as well from within as you wish. If anything feels like it is pushing you out, step out. You are only a guest and must leave if it does not resonate with either of you or another energy for any reason.

To disconnect, just visualize or feel your being and feel yourself shift and expand within your own body and being. Be present, take several deep breaths, feel your body and even hug yourself. You can finish the connection by saying, "thank you for this opportunity to channel through you. I send you pure love, I love you and am grateful for you. We are both coming into balance and new harmony. I ask the cord connecting my heart chakra and third eye with their channel to evaporate into love now. The connection is complete. Alove."

Always ground after a connection is complete. I also recommend writing down any experiences; including visuals, feelings, thoughts, sounds, words, and anything else that was experienced.

Take your time and always be guided by your intuition founded on source love.

# Channeling is Limitless

You are not bound. You are free. I know there are struggles to overcome, things to let go of, programs to transcend, lessons to learn, and love to embrace- but you are free. You are source love incarnated and through that you have the potential and ability to create, channel, transform, transcend, and fully embrace source, love, and the wonder of life- before life, between life, and after life.

Embrace your potential and release all that holds you back. You are doing incredible and I am grateful for how far you've come and for your ability to transform fear into love and reconnect with your most genuine, highest, and loving self.

You are loved, seen, heard, experienced, and felt. Thank you for the love you spread and for your ability to surrender to this love.

You are limitless.

# **Conclusion**

Thank you for joining me in embracing the art of channeling. I appreciate taking the time to be able to assist you on your continuous learning, growing, and transforming journey.

Channeling has so many elements and possibilities. Taking subconscious channeling and fueling conscious awareness to connect further is an incredible way to spread knowledge, peace, and beautiful creations.

If you have any questions, you can always reach out to me through my website, www.magentasunhealing.com or you can speak with me in the heart space, send a telepathic message, and connect journeys if you feel called to.

I feel deep gratitude for all that we are, all that we are embracing, all we are letting go of, and everything we are becoming.

Chloe Moers

Thank you for joining on this journey of life and learning.

We are love <3

# **About the Author/Channeler**

Araya Love (Chloe Moers) is a channeler, author, lover of life, embracer of love, awakener of source love in all life, an energy healer, and always a learner and grower. Her mission is to reconnect all to source love and spread balance throughout Earth and beyond Earth. Her goal is to help Earth be a home for all to live in harmony and peace- free from fear and corruption. She provides interspecies communication, Unconditional Love Reiki (which she channeled from Unconditional Love Consciousness), Fruit Love Healing (channeled from Mother Earth Consciousness), and so many more modalities of energy connection and exchange. Alove and belove <3

Made in United States
North Haven, CT
05 November 2022